# *Time as a Metaphor of History*

THE KRISHNA BHARADWAJ MEMORIAL LECTURE

# Time as a Metaphor of History: Early India

OXFORD
UNIVERSITY PRESS

Oxford University Press is a department of the University of Oxford. It furthers the University's objective of excellence in research, scholarship, and education by publishing worldwide. Oxford is a registered trademark of Oxford University Press in the UK and in certain other countries

Published in India by
Oxford University Press
YMCA Library Building, 1 Jai Singh Road, New Delhi 110001, India



First published 1996
Oxford India Paperbacks 1996
Seventh impression 2011



ISBN-13: 978-0-19-563798-4
ISBN-10: 0-19-563798-4

Typeset by Excellent Laser Typesetter, Pitampura, Delhi 110 034
Printed in India by Sapra Brothers, New Delhi 110 092

For Kaushalya

The Heras Memorial Lectures honour the memory of the Reverend Henry Heras, S.J., who came to India from Spain in 1922 to be Professor of Indian Historical Research Institute, now renamed the Heras Institute of Indian History and Culture. He died in Bombay in 1955, after spending more than half his life digging up India's past in order to display to the world the history and culture of the land he made his own and whose citizen he became. Sponsored by the Heras Society and organized by the Heras Institute, the 1980 Heras Memorial Lectures, seventeenth in the series, were delivered by Professor Romila Thapar, a scholar of the history of ancient India.

# PREFACE

This is an expanded version of the Heras Memorial Lectures on the subject of lineage and state systems in early India, delivered at St. Xavier's College, Bombay in February 1980. I am grateful to Father John Correia-Afonso and the authorities of the Heras Institute and the Heras Society for inviting me to deliver these lectures.

An attempt has been made in these lectures to define the nature of early Indian society during the mid-first millennium B.C. and relate it to the ancient Indian historical tradition in its earliest forms. I have also sought to indicate the particular character of social formations, their genesis and continuity as part of the later Indian social landscape. The data for this book was collected whilst I was on a Jawaharlal Nehru Fellowship during the years 1976 and 1977.

I would like to express my gratitude to my colleagues in the Centre for Historical Studies of the Jawaharlal Nehru University and in particular to Neeladri Bhattacharya, Bipan Chandra, B.D. Chattopadhyaya and Satish Saberwal for their helpful comments on an earlier draft. I would also like to thank Leslie Gunawardana and Sirima Kiribamune at the University of Peradeniya for discussions on the Ceylon Chronicles.

Romila Thapar

# ABBREVIATIONS

| | |
|---|---|
| AISH. | Romila Thapar, *Ancient Indian Social History : Some Interpretations*, New Delhi, 1978 |
| *Ait.* | *Aitareya* |
| *Aṅg.* | *Aṅguttara* |
| *Āpa.* | *Āpastamba* |
| *Brāh.* | *Brāhmaṇa* |
| *D.S.* | *Dharma-sūtra* |
| *D.Śā.* | *Dharma-śāstra* |
| DED. | T. Burrow and M.B. Emeneau, *A Dravidian Etymological Dictionary*, Oxford, 1961 |
| *Dīp.* | *Dīpavaṃsa* |
| *G.S.* | *Gṛhya-sūtra* |
| H.O.S. | Harvard Oriental Series |
| *IHR* | *Indian Historical Review* |
| IRRI | International Rice Research Institute, Philippines |
| *JAOS* | *Journal of the American Oriental Society* |
| *JESHO* | *Journal of the Social and Economic History of the Orient* |
| *Maj.* | *Majjhima Nikāya* |
| *Manu* | *Mānava Dharma-śāstra* |
| *Nik.* | *Nikāya* |
| PED | T.W. Rhys Davids and W. Stede, *Pali-English Dictionary*, P.T.S., London, 1966 |
| *PIHC* | *Proceedings of the Indian History Congress* |
| P.T.S. | Pali Text Society |
| *Ṛg. V.* | *Ṛg Veda* |
| *Śat.* | *Śatapatha* |
| *Sam.* | *Saṁhitā* |
| SBE | Sacred Books of the East |
| *Sm.* | *Smṛti* |
| *Tait.* | *Taittirīya* |
| *Up.* | *Upaniṣad* |
| *Vedic Index.* | A.A. Macdonell and A.B. Keith, *Vedic Index of Names and Subjects*, Delhi, 1967 (reprint) |

# Contents

# Time as a Metaphor of History: Early India*

*This is a much expanded version of the Krishna Bharadwaj Memorial Lecture delivered at Jawaharlal Nehru University in March 1993. I would like to express my appreciation for comments on an earlier draft by David Pingree and Neeladri Bhattacharya.

# I

## The Argument

James Mill, writing what has been described as the hegemonic history of India in the nineteenth century,[1] begins his discussion of what he calls Hindu civilization with the statement:

> Rude nations seem to derive a peculiar gratification from pretensions to remote antiquity. As a boastful and turgid vanity distinguishes remarkably the oriental nations, they have in most instances carried their claims extravagantly high.[2]

Mill was being critical not only of early Indian notions of time and history but also of those Indologists who were attempting a chronological reconstruction of Indian history from these concepts. Yet early Indian notions of time as described in the Manu *Dharmaśāstra*, the *Mahābhārata* and the *Purāṇas*, had attracted much attention even from earlier scholars such as Alberuni in the eleventh century. Alberuni was astute enough to observe the difference between popular views and those of astronomers and mathematicians, even though he otherwise caustically describes Indian astronomy as a mixture of pearls and dung.[3]

This difference was not observed by the early Orientalists, particularly the scholar administrators working in India and commenting on Indian notions of chronology, such as William Jones, Francis Wilford, John Bentley and Thomas Colebrooke. There were also some expectations that unravelling the

[1] R. Inden, 'Orientalist Construction of India', *Modern Asian Studies*, 1986, 20, 3, 401–6.

[2] James Mill, *The History of British India*, Vol. I, London 1858 (fifth ed.), Book II, Chapter 1, 107.

[3] E. C. Sachau, *Alberuni's India*, Delhi 1964 (rep.), I, 25.

traditional knowledge of India might lead to another renaissance, as with the earlier 'discovery' of Greek civilization.[4] Furthermore, such knowledge was also seen as an asset to colonial power in India. Their primary concern was with the texts which they perceived as central to this knowledge, the texts on social codes and on religion. Among these the Manu *Dharmaśāstra* was given priority by local pandits and it is this which they used as their exploratory text into concepts of time and history, gradually extending their interest to other writings.[5]

They searched for works easily recognizable as history backed by at least a skeletal chronology. Such an enterprise yielded little and the unity of Chronos and Clio which they ascribed to the Graeco-Roman world seemed non-existent in Indian civilization. After repeated and unsuccessful attempts at cross-referencing Biblical and Classical information with Indian texts, it was generally conceded that there was an absence of both a sense of history and of the notion of linear time.

At the turn of the eighteenth century and shortly thereafter, the theory which emerged was that the Indian sense of time was entirely cyclic, was tied into an infinity of recurring cycles, and did not therefore recognize historical change; and in the absence of a sense of history there was no differentiation between myth and history. This in part explains the statement by James Mill who endorsed this view of time in early India. Cyclic time was seen as diametrically

[4] R. Schwab, *La Renaissance Orientale*, Paris 1950.

[5] William Jones, 'The Third Discourse', *Asiatic Researches*, 1789, Vol. 1, 354 ff. F. Wilford, 'On the Chronology of the Hindus', in ibid., 345 ff. 1794, Vol. 2, 88–113; 1808, Vol. 5, 241 ff.; J. Bentley, 'Remarks on the Principal Eras and Dates of the Ancient Hindus', in ibid., 1808, Vol. 5, 315 ff.; 'On the Hindu system of Astronomy' in ibid., 1809, Vol. 8, 195 ff. S. Davis, 'On the Indian cycle of sixty years', in ibid., 1794, 3, 289 ff.; H. T. Colebrooke, 'Hindu Astronomy. Mr Colebrooke's Reply to the Attack of Mr Bentley', *Asiatic Journal*, 1826, Vol. 21, 360 ff.

opposite to linear time and linear time was associated with dialectical change. Cyclic time with immense cycles was said to be characteristic of primitive and archaic societies, a particularly galling indictment given the uncomplimentary definition of 'primitive' in those days. This view of Indian time was strengthened by the then current insistence among some Christian sects on a short chronology between the creation of the universe up to the present, many calculating it as a period of about as little as six thousand years.[6] The direction in linear time went from Adam and Eve, via the Jewish prophets to Christ and ultimately to Judgement Day, when the souls of the dead would be awarded everlasting life, either in heaven or hell. This eschatology, relating to the beginning and end of time, was not paralleled in early Indian sources. Linear time therefore came to be viewed as characteristic of the Judaeo-Christian and Islamic traditions. The secularization of linear time in Europe incorporated the notion of change in time and the belief that change was progress as defined in nineteenth-century terms. The challenge to Biblical chronology first posed by geology and biology and later by archaeology, and which was to introduce an infinitely longer time span, was yet to come.[7]

Two hundred years later the received wisdom on the subject remains largely unchanged, even if the reasons for the continuance of these views differ. In the intellectual fashion set by the historian of religion, Mircea Eliade, the fundamental assumptions about time in early India are: that there is an eternal cyclic repetition of time, so huge in concept that human activities become minuscule and insignificant in comparison. Cyclic time is continuous, without a beginning or an end. The cycle returns with unchanging regularity and in unchanging form. This amounts to a refusal of history, for no

[6] S. Toulmin and J. Goodfield, *The Discovery of Time*, Harmondsworth 1967, 92–3.

[7] Ibid., 172 ff.

event can be particular or unique and all events are liable to be repeated in the next cycle. Such a sense of time, based on what has been called an orgy of figures, can only support the philosophic notion of the world being illusory.[8] Time—*kāla*—derived from the root *kal*, to calculate, can also mean to destroy, and is seen in this second meaning as an agency of destruction, resulting in a negative eschatology.

Cyclic time in this argument pertains to the sacred because it is also mythical time, and linear time relates to the profane. The persistence in ascribing cyclic time alone to non-monotheistic religions and ignoring the evidence for other categories of time in the history of their societies was in part because the texts selected emphasized cyclic time in mythology. But the more subtle argument was that such societies live in another time, and this was a device to define the otherness of those societies.

The linear form by contrast was said to have a beginning and an end and emphasized the uniqueness of the particular which made events non-recurring. This was said to liberate history from repetition, deny the reversibility of time, and distinguish history from myth, where myth belonged to a distant time or even timelessness. Whereas change as 'progress' was linked to linear time, it is said to be absent in cyclic time. Thus a close connection was postulated between time concepts as pointers to the centrality of history in society.

This view has very recently been endorsed by some historians of religion, anthropologists and commentators on Indian culture.[9] This is evident in their discussions on perceptions of

[8] M. Eliade, 'Time and Eternity in Indian Thought,' in *Man and Time*, Bollingen Series, xxx, 3. Princeton University Press, New Jersey. *Cosmos and History: The Myth of the Eternal Return*, New York 1959.

[9] An argument derived from grammar states that in Sanskrit the verb from the root **bhu* can be translated both as 'to become' and 'to exist'. Time is conceived statically rather than dynamically. Phrases used for cause and effect read as a compound, effect-and-cause, e.g. *phalahetu*. H. Nakamura, 'Time in Indian and Japanese Thought', in J.T. Fraser (ed.), *The Voices of Time*, London 1986, 77–85.

the past in India, particularly those relating to politics and religion. The argument is often made that because there is no distinction between myth and history in early Indian thought, therefore resort to history even today is irrelevant and meaningless to the Indian mind. Since the dichotomy of cyclic and linear time, projected in the imagery of the phoenix and the ladder, has been basic to this argument, it is worth investigating the forms of time in early Indian texts.

Some attempts have been made to question what has become a stereotype on Indian views of time.[10] Diverse philosophical perceptions of time within the Indian tradition are beginning to be noticed. A study of time in various schools of philosophy points to an evident difference of views where some relate time to the reality of change, others emphasize the distinctiveness of the instant to the point of negating tense, or speak of the subjective construction of sequence, and yet others describe time as flowing like a river which never rests. Such views resemble to some degree the philosophical debates elsewhere between what have been called process philosophers who argue that there is a flow of time and man's advance through it is an important metaphysical fact, and the philosophers of the manifold for whom the flow of time is an illusion and the concept of past, present and future, unreal.

Equally crucial to the discussion is the detailed study of time in India from texts of astronomy and mathematics and what might be called the technology of time in the use of horology, calendars and dating systems. This reveals the construction of knowledge, especially in astronomy and mathematics, and their distance, in some cases, from popular beliefs and also underlines the dialogue between Indian and

[10] A. N. Balslev, *A Study of Time in Indian Philosophy,* Wiesbaden 1983. G. Cardona, 'A Path Still Taken: Some Early Indian Arguments Concerning Time', *Journal of the American Oriental Society,* 1991, 3, 3, 445–64. K. K. Mandal, *A Comparative Study of the Concepts of Time and Space in Indian Thought,* Banaras 1968. A. K. Coomaraswamy, *Time and Eternity,* Ascona 1947.

Greco-Babylonian views.[11] But notions of time are also cultural signals. The reading of these would involve the visualization of the form of time, the degree to which mythical time is distinct from historical time, the association of time with eschatologies, with utopias or with moral and social decline as reflected in golden ages or the decline of *dharma* and the simultaneous use of different time reckonings. It is on these latter aspects that I shall be speaking. They also touch on the question of whether the rhythm of social life can be seen as the basis of categories of time and whether cultures with differing conceptions of time can communicate.[12]

The link between time and history is evident if history is a narrative of human activities of the past, purported to have happened and narrated in the present. Such narrative has an underlying sense of time: it is sequential, moving from the earliest to the most recent. There is a consciousness of change with conjunctures or disjunctures underlying events. Because time is irreversible, the events of the past cannot be altered. However, the assessment of what constitutes an event and its interpretation as history as well as the altering of history through changing causal explanations, is open to discussion. Time concepts and historical change interact in as much as change can be projected as either repetitive, recurrent or periodic, pointing to a wide stretch of time concepts, ranging from what are viewed as the cyclical to the continuously progressive and directional, suggesting a linear form, with many in-between positions such as a wave or a spiral. In terms of eschatology there is an evident difference of form between cyclic and linear time. But not only does cyclic time have a genesis and a predicted termination (as does linear time), it can also encompass segments of time consisting of historical chronologies. Cyclic time does not

[11] D. Pingree, 'Astronomy and Astrology in India and Iran', *Isis*, 1963, 54, 2, 176, 229–46. *Jyotiḥśāstra* (History of Indian Literature Series), Wiesbaden 1981.

[12] J. Fabian, *Time and the Other*, New York 1983.

preclude other categories of time, some more apposite to historical chronology and taking on the functions of linear time. The sharp demarcation between cyclic and linear is made somewhat indistinct by these chronological forms which therefore introduce a range of mediatory positions. The dichotomy weakens if there is a recognition that the one does not negate the other and the two can co-exist. It is also feasible that in some cultures there are grey areas where the two may overlap, as, for example, in Purāṇic time concepts, as I hope to show. These features tended to be ignored in earlier discussions on time and history in India.

## II

## Time-reckoning

Both cyclic and linear time are at one level linked with ideas of cosmology — the theory of the universe as an ordered whole and of the possible laws which govern it. Cosmological time, therefore, relates to the universe, is almost infinite, and where it is cyclic, consists in constructions of many cycles of time, setting out as it were, a calendar for the universe.

Initially those who make the calendar control the reckoning of time. Calendars are part of a larger system of time measurement and calendar-makers were proficient in astronomy. Concepts of time and the theories of astronomers sometimes run parallel, although they are not necessarily interdependent. Astronomers calculated time and conceptualized it. This took the form of extensive computations relating to planetary distances, orbits, asterisms, eclipses and such like, the accumulated knowledge of endless years of observing the night skies and daily shadow readings. These could become patterns in cosmic time. Cosmological time need not be either complete fantasy, or intuitive. It could draw on the existing notions of time current in the calculations of astronomers and mathematicians, although imagination would also be brought into play in the final construct.

Units of time are often initially natural units, such as the cycle of day and night, the cycle of the month based on phases of the moon — the synodic month and lunar fortnights — and the seasonal cycle of the year, starting generally with the spring equinox with segments named after the seasons: what are referred to in the early Indian texts as *ahorātra*, *māsa* and *pakṣa* and the *ṛtus*. The year was also divided into the northern and southern course of the sun on the basis of the solstice —*uttarāyana* and *dakṣināyana*. The lunar day or *tithi* consisted of *muhūrtas*, sometimes refined further to finer measurements as minute as the blinking of an eye.

What may be called ritual time revolved around the cycles of nature. Seasonal rituals often evolved from the routine activities of a given society over the year, e.g. the grazing circuits of herders or the sowing and harvesting periods of cultivators. Some of these were also moments for the gathering of wealth. Ritual time is broadly predictable. Ritual texts sometimes describe the year in terms of the seasons.[13] It comes to be treated as more precise when it is tied to astrology. With reckoning in *muhūrtas* for example, the notion of the auspicious moment comes into existence. Where the ritual is meticulously observed, it suspends the performers of the rituals into a threshold condition where only the parameters of their time-reckoning prevail. Cyclical theories of time arise from the observance of rhythm based on the sequences in relation to the sun and the moon or the seasons.[14] The concept of *ṛta* as a law guiding the universe to ensure regularity and predictability, also derives from the notion of rhythm.

In the early Indian literature, where the need to determine

[13] *Satapatha Brāhmaṇa*, 6. 7. 1. 18; 13. 6. 1. 10–11; 1. 7. 2. 21; 2. 4. 2. 24; *Atharvaveda*, 6. 55. 2.

[14] *Ṛg Veda*, I. 164. 2; 10. 90. 6; 7. 88. 4; for a more poetic rendering, 10. 72.

time was also linked to the efficacy of sacrificial rituals, time is described as a five-spoked wheel, constantly revolving,[15] evoking regular spacing and cyclic movement. In a five-year cycle the solar and lunar calendars were adjusted.

The *nakṣatras* or constellations called for particular attention and this remained a significant activity in early Indian astronomy. The path of the sun and the moon were marked on the basis of a stellar frame. Initially, the five-year cycle was referred to as a *yuga* although later it was extended to a much longer period.[16] The term *yuga*, literally a yoke, is intended to suggest a binding together as an entity. Its usage connected with time refers to a period in which planetary bodies are in conjunction, both at the start and at the end. In the early period the major planets were of course the sun and the moon which had already figured in stellar astronomy. A far more extensive span of time than a five-year cycle was required with planetary movements becoming important. The *yuga* carried not only the notion of a natural cycle and was therefore benign and harmonious but the conjunction of planets carried another meaning, in that it suggested a variety of bi-polarities — good and evil, divine and human, life and death.

Time reckoning was generally based on a luni-solar calendar. The earliest sense of a calendar had to do with time-markers, both of the individual life cycle and involving the environment, which were gradually ritualized. Some had been established in accordance with the lunar calendar with easily comprehensible calculations based on the phases of the moon. The precision of the solar calendar was useful ir agricultural activities and also in horoscopy and in eithe case it became an agency of social control. Measurement of time were required by astrology in the making c horoscopes. These were further activated by the introductior in the early Christian era, of Hellenistic ideas derived fror the obsession with horoscopy and divination among th

[15] *Ṛg Veda*, 1. 164. 13–14

[16] P.V. Kane, *History of Dharmaśāstra*, Poona 1958, Vol. 5, 1, 486.

Graeco-Romans. Predictions based on the signs of the zodiac and the seven-day week — still so prominent in our Sunday newspapers — appear to have been Hellenistic in origin. The urgency to determine time now included the need to know the proper moment for ceremonies and observances — *saṃskāras* — particularly important to the identity of upper castes — as indeed also to improve upon calendars and horoscopes.[17] This became an aspect of ritual time which soon evolved its own forms and rules.

Indian interest in astronomy is revealed in texts dating to the fifth century BC and often included in the category of *Jyotiḥśāstra.* The measurement of time was an important aspect in these studies. The basic unit was initially the five-year *yuga.* Infusions from west Asia introduced further calculations of cyclic time as developed in Greek astronomy based in turn on Babylonian ideas.[18] This interest was an indirect result of the substantial trade and contacts, both overland and maritime, between the eastern Mediterranean and Hellenistic west Asia with northern and western India. Yavanas from the former areas were the visiting traders and some seem to have settled for long periods in India, perhaps even being associated with office.[19] The mingling of Indian and Graeco-Babylonian ideas enhanced activity in astronomy and mathematics in India. This took the form of extensive calculations relating to planets, orbits, eclipses and the like. It has been argued that there was a radical change after *c.* AD 400 when the *Siddhānta-jyotiṣa* replaced the *Vedāṅga-jyotiṣa* and calculations earlier based on stellar and lunar observations now preferred to incorporate planetary motions and solar reckonings.[20]

[17] Pingree, *Jyotiḥśāstra.*

[18] Ibid.

[19] Pingree, *Isis.*

[20] Y. Krishan, 'The Astronomical Revolution in India about AD 400 and its Implications', *Vishveshvaranand Indological Journal,* 1977, 15, 2, 265–84. S.N. Sen, 'Astronomy', in D.M. Bose *et. al.* (eds.), *A Concise History of Science in India,* New Delhi 1971, 81–2.

## III

## Cosmological Time

In the construction of the large cycles of cosmological time the figures used both in cosmology and in astronomy came to be central. In what has been called the *yuga* astronomy of the fifth century AD Indian astronomers calculated that a *kalpa*, the longest period of time, consisted of 4320 million years. The astronomers may have borrowed the notion of a *kalpa* from Puranic sources since they required a long period of time as the basis of their calculations.[21] This raises two questions, one relating to the current theories of cosmological time and the other concerning the dialogue between the authors of a variety of texts.

Cosmological time is described in Manu's *Dharmaśāstra* and in the *Mahābhārata* and is further elaborated upon in the *Purāṇas.* Concepts of time, integrated with ideas on creation, go into the making of what might be called cosmological time. Manu quotes the *mahārṣi* Bhṛgu in describing these concepts which are linked to the notion of the *yugas* calculated in terms of humanly manageable time, as well as the larger unit of divine time associated with Brahmā.[22] It is said that there were six Manus before the present one and this provides one kind of time scale. This is followed by a detailed working out of the smaller units of time from the blinking of an eye to a human year with their equivalents in the enhanced time scale used by the *pitṛs*/ancestors and the *devas*/gods. Given the propensity to classification, different time units were associated with a hierarchy of persons in ascending orders of magnitude. A human month is a day and a night for the ancestors and a human year is the same for the gods. Manu

[21] D. Pingree, personal communication.
[22] Manu, 1. 60–86.

continues with the description of the four *yugas*: the first, the Kṛta lasts for four thousand years with a preceding and subsequent twilight period of four hundred years each. The next three, the Tretā, Dvāpara and Kali, are calculated by reducing one thousand from each with a corresponding reduction of one hundred in the twilight period.

| | | | | | | |
|---|---|---|---|---|---|---|
| Kṛta | 4000 | + | 400 | (X 2) | = | 4800 |
| Tretā | 3000 | + | 300 | (X 2) | = | 3600 |
| Dvāpara | 2000 | + | 200 | (X 2) | = | 2400 |
| Kali | 1000 | + | 100 | (X 2) | = | 1200 |
| | 10,000 | + | 2000 | | = | 12000 |

The total of twelve thousand years constitutes an age of the gods. A thousand of these constitutes a single day of Brahmā and a night of Brahmā is of equal length. The age of Manu, *manvantara*, consists of seventy-one times the age of the gods.

A similar description of the four *yugas* occurs in the *Mahābhārata*, where, at the end of the cycle of four ages or the *mahāyuga*, the Kṛta returns.[23] The emphasis here, as in Manu, is on the change in the character of the four ages accompanied by the increasing decline of *dharma* in each, with a graphic picture of deterioration in the Kali age. At one point it is stated that the world turns upside down in the Kali age.[24] It goes on to list the *mleccha* and other kings who will rule and the list seems to echo the more detailed lists of the *Purāṇas*. Parts of the *Mahābhārata* are regarded as later additions and some of these could well be contemporary with the early *Purāṇas* or at least were borrowing from a common source of ideas, current by the second or third centuries AD.

The theory of the four ages as a conceptualization of cosmological time is more elaborate in the *Purāṇas*, which are generally dated to around the mid-first millennium AD. In the *Viṣṇu Purāṇa*, for instance, it is discussed in the sections on the creation of the world and concepts of cosmography.

[23] Vanaparvan, 186. 17 ff. Śāntiparvan, 224, 6 ff.
[24] Vanaparvan, 186. 28 ff.

The sentiment on the significance of *dharma* remains evident, although there is a greater play with numbers in these texts. The twelve thousand years are treated as divine years and conversion to human years requires multiplication by three hundred and sixty.[25] The length of the *mahāyuga* is therefore calculated as 4,320,000 human years. The *kalpa* which incorporates the *mahāyuga* is calculated as one thousand ages or fourteen *manvantaras.*[26] The *manvantara* is equal to seventy-one times the number of years in a *mahāyuga* with some to spare. This we are told is equal to 852,000 (1200 x 71) divine years or 306,720,000 (360 x 852,000) human years. It has been suggested that this is an imperfect synthesis of more than one independent doctrine and perhaps the *manvantaras* derive from a source different to that of the *mahāyugas.*[27] Kali, the smallest of the ages, extended to 432,000 years. According to one view, the number 432,000 is of Babylonian origin and appears to have been combined with Greek epicycle theory.[28] The *mahāyuga* was a category of time reminiscent of what geologists in the last century termed 'deep time' and perhaps what Fernand Braudel in our century would have recognized as 'la longue durée' — the time of long duration.

The projection of the *kalpa* as cosmological time in non-astronomical texts was almost calculated to defeat any controllable sense of time. Could the mathematical innovations of that period, namely, the concept of the zero and of decimal place value notation have encouraged this formulation of figures and numbers? The magnification to millions was almost a fantasy on ciphers. There is perhaps something ironic in time constructs such as these, playing with the concept of the zero which, as *śūnya,* could refer to emptiness or the void.

[25] *Viṣṇu Purāṇa,* 1. 3. 11 ff.
[26] *Viṣṇu Purāṇa* 3. 2.
[27] A. L. Basham, *The Wonder That was India,* London 1954, 321.
[28] Pingree, *Isis.*

In the cosmology of the *Purāṇas*, the *kalpa* is the period through which creation lasts and is calculated in figures. The dissolution at the end of the *kalpa* occurs when fire and flood engulf creation. In Buddhist, Jaina and Ājīvika texts, the *kalpa* was made unreal not just by the use of the fantasy of figures but also by a spatial description which made it virtually inconceivable. A Buddhist text describes the *kalpa* thus : if there is a mountain in the shape of a cube, measuring one *yojana*[29] and if every hundred years the mountain is brushed with a silk scarf, then the time that is taken for the mountain to be eroded by the scarf is the equivalent of a *kalpa*.[30] Alternatively, if there is a city of iron walls, measuring one cubic *yojana*, and is filled with mustard seeds, and if one seed is taken out every hundred years, the seeds would all be removed before the *kalpa* ended.[31] In Jaina texts the wheel of time, *kālacakra*, is said to consist of zillions of atoms of time, *palyopmas*, calculated to 20 x 10,000,000 (2) x 10 x 10,000,000. The measure of each atom is again described spatially: it is the number of years it would take to empty a cylinder, four miles in length and width, tightly packed with the body hair of humans, if every hundred years a single hair is taken out.[32] The Ājīvika description of a *mahākalpa* states that if there was a river 117,649 times (that is, seven to the seventh power) the size of the Ganga, and if every hundred years one grain of sand is removed from the bed of this imaginary river, the total time for the removal of all the sand will be one *sara*, and 300,000 *saras* equal one *mahākalpa*. (Incidentally, it takes 8,400,000 of these to complete the transmigration of a soul.) This is not the total time of the universe for it continues for infinitely longer.[33] Alternatively, space is also projected as time where the

[29] A *yojana* has been variously calculated and the range extends from two and a half to nine miles.

[30] *Saṃyutta Nikāya*, 2. 180–1.

[31] Ibid., 181–2.

[32] W. Norman Brown, *Man in the Universe*, Berkeley 1966, 77.

[33] A. L. Basham, *History and Doctrine of the Ājīvikas*, London 1951, 253–4.

measurement of the universe with a rope equals the distance which a male celestial being flies in six months at the speed of 2,057,152 *yojanas* in one blinking of the eye.[34] In such reckonings a human life-time would constitute a minuscule moment, described in fact as a dew drop on the tip of a blade of grass when the sun rises or the turning of the chariot wheel which turns by just one place on its rim.[35] Spatial descriptions of extended time are intended to suggest an infinity of time. But since the silk scarf would have disintegrated in the first hundred years or so, spatial descriptions amount to a negation of measurement. It is in this ultimate sense that the Mauryan emperor Aśoka refers to the continuation of his policies by his descendants and by posterity for a *kalpa*.[36] An infinity of time came to represent all of creation.

In Purāṇic cosmology, the *mahāyuga* is more manageable than the *kalpa* since it takes the figures from Manu, converts them to an equivalent in human years and the figures chosen continue to conform to a pattern. Each of the four *yugas* decreases in regulated length with an intermediate dawn and dusk. The Kṛta-yuga extends for 1,728,000 human years, which figure is divisible by 12. The Tretā-yuga decreases in length by a quarter and is 1,296,000 years, and is divisible by 9. The Dvāpara-yuga is reduced by a third and is 864,000 years in length and is divisible by 6. The Kali-yuga, is reduced by a half and is 432,000 years in length and is divisible by 3.[37] The names of the four ages are called after the throw of the four-sided dice, from best to worst. The connection with dice

[34] A. Ghosh (ed.), *Jaina Art and Architecture*, 3 vols., New Delhi 1974–5, 3, 519, n.2. The figure here is 2,857,152, which, it has been said, might be a typographical error since other sources carry 2,057,152.

[35] *Visuddhimagga*, 1. 231,238, quoted in A. K. Coomaraswamy, *Time and Eternity*, Ascona 1947.

[36] Fourth Major Rock Edict. J. Bloch, *Les Inscriptions d'Asoka*, 1950, 100. Fifth Major Rock Edict, Ibid., 102.

[37] *Viṣṇu Purāṇa* 1. 3. 11 ff; 6. 1. *Matsya Purāṇa*; 142 ff. In some texts the fourth age had been called *āskanda* or *tiṣya*. Kane, *History of Dharmaśāstra*, 3, 887.

introduces the element of chance into what may otherwise appear to be pre-ordained. Play at dice is opposed to a permanent accumulation of wealth and has a levelling effect, sometimes even circulating that which is scarce. Transactions of exchange tend to get neutralized as the game proceeds.[38] Was time seen as playing a similar role?

This construction of a time scale has many interesting facets. Orderliness of a mathematical kind was basic to the concept. The shortening of the length of each *yuga* is in descending arithmetical progression. The numbers have a mathematical link as in figures such as 60, 72, 84, 360, 1200, 432,000. The numbers also echo a variety of sources; 432,000 is said to be the number of the syllables in the *Ṛg Veda* and the number in the three Vedic texts is double that, 864,000.[39] It is unlikely that a precise syllable count was made of the *Vedas.* Were these numbers in turn picked up from other sources? In Mesopotamian schedules, apart from the use of the basic sexigesimal system, the final sums are multiples of the same integer which in India came to be associated with the sum of divine years in a cosmic cycle. The multiplication of 1200 by 360 yields 432,000. This was also the time period given for the pre-diluvian kings in Babylonian sources as recorded by Berossos, the Babylonian historian of the third century BC [40] During the previous centuries Achaemenid west Asia had encroached on north-western India and possibly the number 72, which was basic to Biblical and Babylonian chronology, became popular in Indian time calculations. From the Babylonian perspective too, some numerals such as 7,9,12,360 were seen as endowed with a special magical

[38] J. Woodburn, 'Egalitarian Societies', *Man,* n.s., 1982, 17, 431–51. Some later texts raise objections to gambling, presumably when the accumulation of wealth is not to be questioned. Baudhāyana, *Dharmasūtra,* 2, 15–16.

[39] *Śatapatha Brāhmaṇa,* 10. 4. 2. 22–5. Kane, 5, 1, 689–90.

[40] P. Schnabel, *Berossos und die Babylonisch-Hellenistische Literatur,* Leipzig 1923, 261–3. D. Pingree, "The Purāṇas and Jyotiḥśāstra: Astronomy", *Journal of the American Oriental Society,* 1990, 110, 2, 275.

potency and were therefore treated differently from figures in mathematics.[41] Yet these figures occur in astronomy and the similarities may not be altogether accidental. It would seem that such figures may have been travelling back and forth between India and west Asia as they continued to do into later centuries.

## IV

## The Authors

Numbers such as these were not unfamiliar in the calculations of astronomers at this time but there was not always a uniform agreement on the figures basic to calculations. One at least of the astronomers did not accept, for purposes of his own calculations, the unequal length of the four *yugas*. Āryabhaṭa in the fifth century AD was singled out even in later times as having argued in favour of four ages of equal length of 1,080,000 years.[42] A subsequent astronomer, Brahmagupta, disagreed with this and endorsed the alternative figures closer to the cosmological scheme. The cosmography of a flat earth was also rejected in favour of a sphere. In the mid-eighth century the astronomer Lalla refuted what he found unacceptable in Purāṇic texts.[43] Still later, Vaṭeśvara disagreed with Brahmagupta and supported Āryabhaṭa.[44] There appears to have been some divergence among astronomers as also between them and the authors of the *Purāṇas*.

What then was the nature of discourse among the authors of the *Purāṇas* constructing an imaginary cosmos and the astronomers after the mid-first millennium AD? Were the

[41] F. Cumont, *Astrology and Religion among Greeks and Romans*, New York 1912/1960 (rep), 18, 62.

[42] Alberuni, 1, 373–4.

[43] Lalla, *Śiṣyadhīvṛddhidatantra*. D. Pingree, 'The Purāṇas and Jyotiḥśāstra: Astronomy', *Journal of the American Oriental Society*, 1990, 110, 2, 274–80.

[44] S.N. Sen, 97.

*paurānikas*, using the immensity of the figures and resorting to mathematical patterns, attempting to intimidate those who listened to the recitation of these texts? Where the numerals were common to the *Purāṇas* and to astronomy, even if there was no logical connection between the two categories of knowledge, a claim to further authenticity on the part of the *paurānikas* would seem to be implicit. Was there an intellectual divergence among the authors of various categories of texts for, although they were all *brāhmaṇas,* they were trained differently and performed different functions? Although they belonged to the same *varṇa* there was within it a professional differentiation which had social dimensions. The mere fact of a brahmanical authorship of the various texts need not assume an identity of content and purpose, and there may well have been ideological differences.

Interestingly the incorporation of cosmic time is particularly emphasized in some texts, such as the *Mahābhārata* and certain *Purāṇas* which are believed to have originally had a link with bards. The later written versions of the texts are said to have been revised by the *brāhmaṇas*. The Bhṛgu *brāhmaṇas* are sometimes associated with this and they have a curiously ambivalent social position in the *brāhmaṇa varṇa*.[45] Were the authors of the *Purāṇas* unable to keep abreast of the astronomers and mathematicians who had incorporated Hellenistic and other systems into their theories? For example, Yavanarāja Sphujidhvaja states in the third century AD that in the previous century Yavaneśvara translated a Greek astrological text, now lost, into Sanskrit as the *Yavana-jātaka*. In the fourth century, Mīnarāja, who also refers to himself with the title of Yavanarāja, wrote the *Vṛddha-yavana-jātaka*. These texts are quoted by Indian astronomers.[46] It may be said

[45] V.S. Sukthankar, 'The Bhṛgus and the Bhārata: A Text-historical Study', *Annals of the Bhandarkar Oriental Research Institute*, 18, 1–76. F.E. Pargiter, *The Purāṇa Text of the Dynasties of the Kali Age*, Delhi 1975 (rep), 77 ff. R.P. Goldman, *Gods, Priests and Warriors*, New York 1977.

[46] D. Pingree, *The Yavanajātaka of Sphujidhvaja, I*, Cambridge, Mass. 1978. Introduction.

in passing that there is a virulent attack on the Yavanas, the people from the west, in a text with the curious title of *Yuga Purāṇa,* although interestingly, the expertise of the Yavanas in astronomy is conceded.[47] Varāhamihira states that although the Yavanas are *mlecchas,* and therefore outside the social pale, nevertheless, given their knowledge of astronomy, they are honoured as *ṛṣis.*[48] If there was a change from calculations based on the constellations and the moon to planetary and solar astronomy around AD 400, it may have also encouraged divergent thinking.

## V

## Time and the Decline of *Dharma*

The answers to some of these questions may also lie in the insistence on social and moral decline underlined in Purāṇic cosmological time. This was consistently endorsed as characteristic of change over the four ages. Sometimes the description of the *yugas* is merely a prelude to the lengthy statements on the reversal, from the brahmanical perspective, of norms and mores, which reversal characterizes the Kali age. The gradual decline of *dharma* is stated both directly and in symbols. The utopian conditions of the first age, also sometimes referred to as Satya, the age of Truth, diminish slowly until nothing of the utopia is left in the Kaliyuga. Thus in the first age people live to 400 years, never suffering from disease or from insecurity. By contrast, in the fourth age, life expectancy comes down to 100 years and the

[47] D.C. Sircar, *Studies in the Yuga Purāṇa and other Texts,* Delhi 1974. J.E. Mitchiner, *The Yuga Purāṇa,* Calcutta 1986.

[48] *Bṛhatsamhitā,* 2. 32. M. Ramakrishna Bhat (ed.), *Varāmihira's Bṛhatsamhitā,* Delhi 1981.

*śūdras* are in the ascendent.[49] In the Kṛta age men lived as long as they chose to and procreation did not require sexual activity, but in the Kali age marriage became necessary.[50] In another text life-expectancy drops from 30,000 in the Kṛta age to 100 years in the Kali age.[51] In the Jaina tradition the start of the cycle was evident by the tallness of humans, a man's height being six miles and the number of his ribs being 256. Gradually both the height and the number of ribs decreased until in the present era, life expectancy is down to 125, the number of ribs to 16 and the height to seven cubits (*hastas,* of about eighteen inches). And this will decrease further in the future.[52] Or there is the image of *dharma,* sometimes likened to a bull, which stands on four legs in the first age and drops a leg in each subsequent age, symbolizing the decline in moral and social order.[53] The present is invariably an age of evil when social mores are turned upside-down. This was in part the expected decline in the decreasing cycle where human actions would relate to the quality of the *yuga.*

It could also be interpreted as resentment at royal patronage to non-brahmanical ideologies, for the *brāhmaṇas* were not yet at the forefront as recipients of material prosperity. The Kaliyuga symbolizes the breaking down of caste ranking as a determining feature of social activities. Mention is made of *mleccha* rulers, corrupt *brāhmaṇas* and upstart *śūdras* taking on the airs of *brāhmaṇas* and performing priestly functions. Equally important, the subordination of women, so crucial to the continuance of caste, disintegrates and results particularly in sexual freedom for women.[54] This

[49] Manu 1.83. Kane, 3,244 ff; 892 ff. *Viṣṇu Purāṇa,* 6. 1 and 2. *Mahābhārata,* Vanaparvan, 148. 10ff ; 186. 23ff.

[50] *Mahābhārata,* Śāntiparvan, 200, 35 ff.

[51] *Aṅguttara Nikāya,* 4, 156.

[52] S. Stevenson. *The Heart of Jainism,* New Delhi 1970 (rep.), 273 ff.

[53] Manu 1. 81–2, 8, 16.

[54] *Viṣṇu Purāṇa,* 6. 1. 10 ff. *Mahābhārata,* Vanaparvan, 188. 10–93.

is unlikely as a description of an actual situation and the Kaliyuga is here being constructed as the antonym to an ideal brahmanical society. Historical evidence points to social change in the latter part of the first millennium AD but not of the kind envisaged in the description of the Kali age. For example, *brāhmaṇa* ascendency was established through extensive royal grants of land to a variety of *brāhmaṇas* but this did not lead to a rescinding of the picture of the Kali age. The idyllic community of the distant past is expected to return but in the equally distant future. But the *yugas* were not merely a measurement in time. Conflicting views among the authors of the texts setting out the norms could be sorted out by arguing that a particular interpretation, no longer current, was prevalent in the previous *yuga*.[55] Substantial changes in customary laws and rituals explained as Kalivarjaya are in effect related to problems arising from social change in the latter part of the first millenium AD.[56] The horrors of the Kaliyuga are recited repeatedly from this period onwards. The coming of the tenth *avatāra* of Viṣṇu, Kalkin — a name also associated with time — will usher in a new age. Kalkin will destroy the *melcchas*, the rulers and the heretics.[57] There is a touch of the messianic in the coming of Kalkin.

Slotted into this theory of the decline of *dharma* is also the notion of transmigration or metempsychosis — *karma* and *saṃsāra*. The cyclic notion is reinforced by the idea of transmigration, with the *ātman* or soul being constantly reborn. Much earlier, the *Upaniṣads* had tied together the notions of time, the planets and rebirth in the argument that after death the soul travels along two major paths — the *devayāna* or path of the gods and the *pitṛyāna* or path of the ancestors. Those who were free from rebirth took the former path which was associated with the sun and led the soul to the world of Brahmā and eternal life. Those who had to undergo

[55] Kane, 3, 865 ff.
[56] Ibid. 926 ff, 966 ff.
[57] *Viṣṇu Purāṇa*, 4. 24. 98. P.V. Kane, 3.923 ff.

rebirth took the path of the ancestors, associated with the moon, and eventually returned to earth.[58] Implicit in this notion are certain consequences. There is the inevitability of death with which time comes to an end. Religious beliefs attempt to reverse this inevitability by proposing rebirth through many lives, or, as in the Semitic religions, everlasting life in heaven or hell subsequent to Judgement Day. In either case, one cannot escape the consequences of one's actions. Therefore, if present action determines the future, then the past, present and future are inextricably linked.[59] This kind of thinking was in turn incorporated into horoscopy.[60]

The deterministic procession of time towards decline is arrested and challenged by the individual *karma* and this idea became even more significant with the notion that *bhakti* — devotion to and sharing in the grace of the deity — was an avenue of release from rebirth. It is at the human level that the immensity of time can be challenged for in its totality time is almost beyond human comprehension. There is a near dialectical relationship between the individuality of *karma* and the virtual inevitability of the time cycle. The decline in morality in the fourth age acts as a peg on which one can hang one's inability to change the course of events particularly if it points towards retrogression. But the four ages need not be perceived as enclosed units for it is said that a king's conduct characterizes the identity of the age and this ties ethics and social behaviour to time.[61] Ultimately the possibility of the return of the cycle provides the necessary optimism for continuing human action and also gives a meaning to human action in the past: it makes history necessary.

The change, implicit in each *yuga*, is so firmly emphasized that one may wonder how the idea that cyclic time did not

[58] *Bṛhadāraṇyaka Upaniṣad*, 6. 2. 15ff. *Chāndogya* 5. 10; 10. 1. 2; 4. 15.

[59] P.V. Kane, *History of Dharmaśāstra*, Poona 1946, 3, 923 ff. 5, 484 ff. Balslev.

[60] Kane, 5, 484ff. The sixth-century text, the *Bṛhajjātaka*, links horoscopy to *karma* and *punar janma*.

[61] Manu, 9. 301–2. *Mahābhārata*, Śāntiparvan, 70. 6.

conceive of change took root in modern views on the subject. Admittedly, in the existing *mahāyuga*, the notion of change in the Purāṇic version is towards decline and not towards progress although the conduct of the king can change this direction. The linking of a particular period of time with social change marks a difference between the Puranic cosmological time with its implications for human society, and time as conceived in astronomy. Jayasiṃha points to the decline of planetary motions as the *mahāyuga* progresses, but this may be seen as a different concept of decline from the Puranic.[62] The figures from astronomy are relatively value-free, arising out of computations of time. This difference is important to the relationship between time and history.

## VI

## Myth and History

The induction of cosmological time into the early *Purāṇas* raises the question of the relationship of myth to history and it is to this that I would now like to turn. It has been argued that myths narrate events in primordial, atemporal moments which constitute sacred time and differ from the continuous profane time of daily routines. Therefore, by narrating myths profane time is abolished.[63] The question then is whether this was true of the treatment of time in the *Purāṇas*. Although not stated directly, was there at least the suggestion that a differentiation was being perceived between different forms of time and the assessment of past events ? Was cosmological time seen as mythic time ? Was mythic time segregated

[62] D. Pingree: personal communication.

[63] Eliade, *Cosmos and History : the Myth of the Eternal Return*, 112 ff. 'Time and Eternity in Indian Thought', in *Man and Time*, Bollingen Series, xxx, 3.

from chronological time in narrating the past? Was this segregation seen as a mechanism for separating myth and history?

Among the *Purāṇas*, the *Viṣṇu Purāṇa* observes what is described as the ideal format in its five sections and one of the five provides an overview of the perceived past. This is the *vamśānucarita* which narrates the succession of those who ruled and can be divided into three distinct, although unequal, sections.[64] The narrative begins with the briefest reference back to the previous sections of the text which describe the genesis of the universe, giving details of creation, of time cycles as both the *mahāyugas* and the *manvantaras,* and of cosmography. The Manus are mentioned in passing, spanning immense cycles of time. They have no association with specific events nor do they indicate any particular social condition.

In the reign of the seventh Manu there occurs the great Flood from which Manu is saved by Viṣṇu in his fish incarnation, the *matsya-avatāra.*[65] Manu and the seven *ṛṣis* are placed in a boat and the boat is tied to the single horn of the fish (the incarnated Viṣṇu) and they go through the waters of the Flood and are lodged safely on the top of a mountain (in some texts, this is Mount Meru, the *axis mundi*). When the Flood subsides, creation starts anew. The story of the Flood is in many ways similar to the Mesopotamian story. The earliest version occurs in the *Śatapatha Brāhmaṇa* and may reflect a borrowing from west Asia where there are still earlier versions of the story.[66] The Flood acts as a time marker separating the period of the Manus from that of the *kṣatriya rājās* who followed. Floods have a dual symbolism of

[64] *Viṣṇu Purāṇa* 4. Romila Thapar, 'Genealogical Patterns as Perceptions of the Past', *Studies in History,* 1991, n.s., 7, 1, 1–36.

[65] This is narrated in great detail, for obvious reasons, in the opening chapters of the *Matsya Purāṇa,* but not in the *Viṣṇu Purāṇa.*

[66] *Śatapatha Brāhmaṇa,* 1. 8. 1. 1 ff. W.G. Lambert and A.R. Millard. *Atrahasis,* Oxford 1969.

water washing away that which is physically present as well as the silt deposited from the Flood providing a fresh beginning in the space which had been flooded.

In the next and second section of the chapter on succession, the measurement of time changes radically from the cyclic time associated with the Manus and the *manvantaras*, to reckoning time as generations through lengthy genealogies. Cosmological time appears to be now distanced from the lists of descent by the use of a time schedule seemingly more manageable in human terms. I would like to suggest that both the Flood and the change to reckoning in generational time through genealogies are mechanisms of demarcating myth in cosmological time from that which occupies the ambiguous area approaching history.

The listing of generations in the *Viṣṇu Purāṇa* begins with the description of Manu's progeny who are said to be the ancestors of the earliest *kṣatriyas.* Among them the most important are Ikṣvāku who initiates the Sūryavaṃśa or Solar lineage, and Iḍā or Ilā, whose androgynous form is suggested and from whose female self are descended another group of *kṣatriyas* identified as the Candravaṃśa or Lunar lineage. These two descent groups are also integrated into the two epics, for the heroes of the *Rāmāyaṇa* are of the Sūryavaṃśa and those of the *Mahābhārata* are of the Candravaṃśa. The association of the sun and the moon with these descent groups carries a rich symbolism which touches on many facets, but for our purposes here it is significant as a parallel to the calendars in use. Time reckoning in this section is characterized by the sequence of generations and is for all practical purposes an exercise in linear time, although a location within the *yuga* system forms the ultimate time frame.

The term used for a succession list of any kind or a genealogy is *vaṃśa,* derived from the name for bamboo. This is an appropriate image where each node marks a new generation of growth. This in itself would suggest linear time. Genealogies have a tentative beginning in the early chapters of the epics, but the construction of a narrative in genealogical form comes into its own in the early *Purāṇas*. This may be called a construction since it covers almost a hundred generations and such an immense genealogy could hardly have been an authentic record.[67] It is however possible that genealogies, not as authentic descent lists but as narratives of the past, existed in earlier centuries and were incorporated into and reorganized in the *Purāṇas*. Thus Megasthenes, the ambassador from the Hellenistic Seleucid kingdom in Iran, is quoted as saying that the Indians count kings over 153 (or 154 according to the later Roman historian, Pliny) generations or 6451 years and three months from the time of Alexander (in the fourth century BC.), going back to the earliest settlement which it is claimed was established by Bacchus.[68]

The genealogies in themselves are not invariably authentic but they incorporate patterns and narratives which are indicative of a recognition of particularities. For example, the Sūryavaṃśa pattern is the history of descent from father to eldest son alone, generally suggestive of primogeniture, whereas the Candravaṃśa often lists more than a single line of descent among brothers, suggestive perhaps of a segmentary lineage system. The genealogies are therefore not necessarily intended as historically accurate — and this would be evident from the variants in the name and position in the descent list among the different *Purāṇas* — but they do seem to be making a statement about how the past was perceived and these perceptions may be intended as the more authentic history.

The descent list of the Sūryavaṃśa peters out. The Candravaṃśa, purporting to record segmentary clans,

[67] F.E. Pargiter, *Ancient Indian Historical Tradition*, London 1922.

[68] Solin, 52. 5 ; Pliny, *Natural History*, 6. 21. 4–5. Arrian in the *Indika IX*, gives the figures of 153 generations, from Dionysus to Candragupta, and 6042 years. J.W. McCrindle, *Ancient India as Described by Megasthenes and Arrian*, London 1877, 115, 203.

continues to the grand finale of the *Mahābhārata* war in which virtually all the clans are directly or indirectly involved and few survive. The catastrophic war, described as the end of the glorious age of the *kṣatriyas,* becomes another time-marker. If the choice of a time marker is a signpost to the culture, it would seem appropriate that the *kṣatriya* clans would terminate their activities in a war. The keeping of genealogies and reckoning by generations, whether factual or fictive, are important to lineage-based societies where rank is determined by birth and such clans claim dominant social status.[69] Genealogical time becomes important to the process of legitimation. Earlier generations can be stretched back into a remote past or claims to heroic ancestry can be telescoped so as to be placed closer to the claimant.

That both the Flood and the *Mahābhārata* war were viewed as significant time-markers is indicated by the uncertainty as to where the start of the Kaliyuga should be placed.[70] The *Viṣṇu Purāṇa* states that the Kali age began after the war,[71] although some other texts place it earlier, thus eliminating a precise time. However, the start of the Kaliyuga in the *Viṣṇu Purāṇa* is located with reference to a constellation, thus implicitly suggesting a point in time. The astronomers, for reasons of facilitating calculations, worked out the date of the Kaliyuga as equivalent to 3102–1 BC. This was the date which came to be adopted in inscriptions and histories as well where precise dates were required.[72] But in the *Purāṇas* it was viewed more as the condition of society than as a precise point in time. Cosmological time did not debar other forms of time reckoning, perhaps more realistic and therefore liable to be subsumed in cosmological time.

[69] Romila Thapar, *From Lineage to State,* Delhi 1984.

[70] Kane, 5, 687.

[71] *Viṣṇu Purāṇa,* 4. 24. 104–7, 113. F.E. Pargiter, *The Puranic Texts of the Dynasties of the Kali Age,* Delhi 1975 (rep.), 61.

[72] Aihole inscription of Pulakeśin II, *Epigraphia Indica,* 6.7. This is a neat inclusion of the shorter Śaka era reckoning within the span starting with the Kaliyuga. Varāhamihira, *Bṛhatsamhitā,* 13, 3. J.F. Fleet, 'The Kaliyuga of 3102 BC', *Journal of the Royal Asiatic Society,* 1911, 479–96 and 675–98. Kalhaṇa, *Rājataraṅgiṇī* 1. 51–6.

Subsequent to the *Mahābhārata* war, in the third section of the chapter on succession in the *Viṣṇu Purāṇa*, the narrative dramatically changes its tense from the past to the future and becomes a lengthy prediction of events. This would seem to be another example of pointing to historical change, through adopting a new category of time. What follows soon after is a listing of dynasties which is a change from the earlier lists of descent groups and within these dynasties the succession of rulers with, in some *Purāṇas*, their regnal years. Time periods and regnal years of the initial dynasties are obviously exaggerated but the lists gradually become more credible. The geneological form continues and the succession of dynasties as a new pattern of chronology is suggestive of linear time. The generational form is however limited to the names within the dynasty. Dynasties as such are generally not related to each other and in some cases it is specifically mentioned that the successor dynasty began as a *bhṛtya* or in the service of the earlier one.[73] The association with the Kaliyuga is less in terms of a point in time and more as an explanation of why, when the *kṣatriya* clans died out, it was possible not only for *śūdras* to rule — which at that time was contrary to the norms — but it was also possible later for kings to be from socially unacceptable groups, such as the *mlecchas* or those outside the social pale, the *vrātya-kṣatriyas* or degenerate *kṣatriyas* and the Śabaras and Pulindas who were forest dwellers and therefore regarded as primitive and beyond the boundaries of caste society. Prophesying history becomes a mechanism for using the past to lay claim to controlling the future. But the use of the future tense had its obvious limitation, namely, that the prophecy had to stop at the point when the text was composed, in this case towards the mid-first millennium AD.

Within the narrative of the chapter on succession in the *Viṣṇu Purāṇa* there is a demarcation of three periods based on various categories of time. The first is remote, that of the Manus and their large time cycles ; the second has a faint

[73] *Viṣṇu Purāṇa*, 4. 24. 43. Pargiter, *The Puranic Texts*... 38.

continuity from the first but focuses on a changed chronological pattern through genealogical or generational time; and finally, subsequent to the *Mahābhārata* war there follows a period of dynastic time reckoning. Cosmological time in this context, although all-encompassing, is nevertheless viewed as distant and possibly as mythical time. Dynastic time in effect takes the functional form of historical chronology. A distinction between myth and history, although not stated in these terms, appears to have been perceived. The coming of the Kaliyuga heralds a major change in time-reckoning. The forms in which time is depicted seem to be making a statement about historical change.

## VII

## Historical Time

But let us not forget that in the immensity of the time cycle we are still at the threshold of the Kaliyuga of 432,000 years. A more realistic kind of time reckoning was therefore also required. This drew on actual historical needs and is in some ways related to the last section of the chapter on succession in the *Viṣṇu Purāṇa.* Cosmological time did not debar other forms of time reckoning, even those perhaps with shorter spans and therefore liable to be subsumed in the compass of cosmological time. These may be viewed as fragmentary arcs within the cycle which take on the role of linear time. The dichotomy between cyclic and linear becomes increasingly vague.

An innovation of a new kind drawing on both astronomy and history provided another set of time markers and inaugurated a system of timereckoning which was distinctively different. This has curiously been overlooked by those insisting on early Indian time concepts being exclusively cyclic. The use of eras as well as dating by regnal years had gained currency, simultaneously with activity in astronomy and cosmology. This is particularly evident in documents concerning those in political authority. Regnal years go back to the earliest historical inscriptions, the edicts of the Mauryan emperor Aśoka, issued in the third century BC. Regnal years and eras point to time reckoning being based on a precise point in time and the starting point of the reckoning being known.

Linear time came to be used more extensively from the Christian era onwards in a variety of ways. Dynastic lists gradually came into circulation. Biographies of those in power, and especially kings, took as their time bracket the dynasty to which the subject of the biography belonged, relating him both to a description of origins and to early rulers, but focussed on the major activities of particular kings. The use of historical eras located kings and dynasties more firmly in time. The event or the person became a point in time and became stable within that tradition. The use of eras gained currency and this is particularly evident in documents emanating from those in authority.

The system of eras, according to some scholars, grew out of points in time invented to facilitate calculations in astronomy. The Kṛta era of 58 BC, also known as the Mālava era, and later, from the eighth century AD referred to as the Vikrama era, has been claimed as commemorating an historical event, although the suggestion has also been made that it may be associated with astronomy.[74] The term *saṁvatsara* came to be used for era. Other commonly used

[74] D.C. Sircar, *Indian Epigraphy*, Delhi 1965, 251 ff. F. Kielhorn, 'Examination of Questions Connected with the Vikrama Era,' *The Indian Antiquary*, 1891, 20, 397–414. If there is a link with astronomy, it may be suggested that Mālava may have been associated with Ujjain, the meridian for some calculations in astronomy. Both Bivar and Fussman have associated the Vikrama era with Azes I. A.D.H. Bivar, 'The Azes Era and the Indravarma Casket', *South Asian Archaeology, 1979*, Berlin 1981, 369–76. G. Fussman, 'Nouvelles Inscriptions Śaka: ère d'Eucratide, ère d'Azes, ère Vikrama, ère de Kaniṣka', *BEFEO*, 1980, 67, 1–43.

eras were the Śaka (AD 78), the Kalacuri Cedi (AD 247–8), the Gupta (AD 319–20) and so on. Subsequent to this there is a mushrooming of new eras all over the sub-continent.

The historical use of an era sometimes associated it with either an accession — such as the Gupta era — or with being a status symbol adding lustre to a reign — as in the case of the Cālukya-Vikrama era. At the functional level, eras introduced more precise dating in official documents. But this was not the only significance of using an era. More importantly, it helped separate cosmological time reckoning from the functional, although the former was not discarded. That the fashion for and computation of eras began from the use of methods influenced by Hellenistic astronomy may be one explanation, but it was also related to other changes which were conducive to the establishing of eras.

Dynasties are associated with monarchies and these in turn presuppose the emergence of a state system. The adoption of a short-spanned and more precise time reckoning associated with those in authority, was encouraged by the establishing of a state. This time reckoning, even when encompassed by the longer spans of cosmological time, introduces a precision which lends strength to the authority of the state. The need to maintain state records and official documents, not to mention texts legitimizing persons and institutions, tended to make the history of those in authority more evident. The time dimension of these was effectively linear. Elements of linear time in the context of early India have therefore a different origin from linear time in the Judaeo-Christian tradition, where it is linked to the sacred.

The use of historical eras may have been partially influenced by the parallel tradition of the Buddhists where major events came to be dated in the number of years from the *Mahāparinirvāṇa* or the passing away of the Buddha. The date for this, it was believed, was carefully recorded and after the removal of some discrepancies in late texts, most scholars, basing themselves on the sources in question, accepted 486 or 483 BC as the date of the death of the Buddha. Recently this date has been questioned and it is being suggested that the Buddha may have lived and died almost a century later.[75] What is significant, however, is that within particular Buddhist traditions there was a stable date. Perhaps because of this stable date, chronicles written by Buddhist monks, for example, display a sharper sense of time and relate all events to this date, which is associated with a historical person. Perhaps the historicity of the Buddha and the establishing of the *saṅgha* separated myth from history, although the narrative of individual events was often wrapped in myths. Buddhism maintained monastic institutions, the chronology and history of which were, in some cases, recorded when they became centres of power. Sectarian breakaways, of which there were many, could claim greater legitimacy if they placed themselves in relation to this history. Proselytizing ideologies claim legitimacy, both from myth and presumed history. There was also, for instance in the Sri Lankan Chronicles, such as the *Dīpavaṃsa* and the *Mahāvaṃsa*, a reconstruction of regnal years and events relating to the earliest narrative about the history of Sri Lanka, in order to corelate events in Sri Lanka with the biography of the Buddha. Later the history of the *saṅgha* was integrated with the political history of Sri Lanka and in its initial stages even with the rule of the Mauryas in India.[76] This became necessary because Aśoka came to be projected as legitimizing the sect of the Theravāda and the authors of these chronicles were Theravāda monks.

The adoption of historical eras or regnal years meant that official documents began to carry dates. Among these documents are inscriptions which are in effect the annals of

[75] H. Bechert (ed.), *The Dating of the Historical Buddha*, 2 vols., Gottingen 1991.

[76] L.S. Perera, 'The Pali Chronicles of Ceylon', in C.H. Philips, *Historians of India, Pakistan and Ceylon*, London 1961.

Indian history. Issued by individual rulers and by members of the ruling class in the main, they include votive records relating to grants and gifts as well as statements of events, especially those important to politics and administration. Some carry brief histories of the dynasty as a prelude to the specific action recorded. The date is precise and includes the era or the regnal year of the ruler, the season, month, fortnight and the day. It follows calendrical requirements for a date and this enables the calculation, for example, of its equivalence in the Gregorian calendar. Facility in the use of calendars would have required professional expertise. Hence the continuing importance of the astrologer, who, apart from horoscopy, sustained his authority by keeping track of both lunar and solar calendars.[77] The status of the astrologer in the earlier texts remained low even within the *brāhmaṇa varṇa* and he was excluded from *śrāddha* ceremonies, but interestingly, the later *Bṛhatsamhitā*, endorsing astrology, contradicts this and refers to the astrologer as the *sāmvatsara* and requires that he be honoured as the chief guest at a *śrāddha*.[78]

Precision in dating inscriptional documents became necessary because they were often official statements or legal charters. The recording of a precise moment requires a context and a location. Alternatively, depending on the nature of the grant, it may have been required to negate the effect of something inauspicious such as an eclipse. In such cases the precision in dating had to do with an astrologically appropriate moment. Despite the interest in horoscopes, history became more recognizable and in its use of time reckoning, it gradually sloughed off some of its earlier ritual context.

Apart from inscriptions, other categories of records such as biographies and dynastic and regional chronicles — the *caritas* and the *vaṃśāvalis* — articulated views on the past.

[77] Kane, 3, 126. D.C. Sircar, *Indian Epigraphy*, Delhi 1965, 227.

[78] Manu, 3. 162; 6. 50. Baudhāyana 2. 1. 2. 16. *Arthaśāstra*, 9. 4. 25–6. *Bṛhatsamhitā*, 2. 6 ; 2. 31, quoted in Y. Krishan.

These evolved into genres of literature and borrowed from the courtly literary style but their functions, as records and as legitimizing those in power were new and significant. Biographies, particularly of kings, took as their time bracket the dynasty to which the subject of the biography belonged. They focussed on what they assessed as the more significant events of the reign. Where authorship is specific, the recording of time also tends to be more specific. The composition and records of poets and bards, sometimes close to the court, but often closer to popular sentiment, were yet another form of legitimation, but could occasionally contest the official version of events.[79]

The *caritas* and *vaṃśāvalis* drew, when they chose to, on the *Purāṇas* but their view of the past was not identical to that of the *Purāṇas.*[80] Examples of such *caritas* are the *Harṣacarita* of Bānabhaṭa, the biography of the seventh century ruler Harṣavardhana, or Bilhaṇa's *Vikramānkadeva-carita* which focuses on Vikramāditya VI, an eleventh century Cālukya king.[81] Some of the lengthier inscriptions carried narratives of the dynasty and among these is the tenth century Khajuraho inscription set up by Dhaṅga for his father, Yaśovarman.[82] This is an official version of the origins and early history of the Candella dynasty. Two contested versions are known : one refers to their origins and caste status which is placed low and the other is an alternative view of the reign of one of the kings from the perspective of a popular ballad.[83] An example

[79] Romila Thapar, *Clan, Caste and Origin Myths in Early India,* Simla 1992.

[80] Romila Thapar, 'Society and Historical Consciousness: the *Itihāsa-Purāṇa* Tradition', in S. Bhattacharya and Romila Thapar (eds.), *Situating Indian History,* Delhi 1986, 353–83.

[81] For references to other such biographies, see V.S. Pathak, *Ancient Historians of India,* Bombay 1966. A.K. Warder, *An Introduction to Indian Historiography,* Bombay 1972.

[82] *Epigraphia Indica,* 1, 122.

[83] *Pṛthvirāj-rāso* by Candbardai refers to the low origin of the Candellas and is written from the point of view of their then enemies, the Cahamānas. The *Ālhākhaṇḍ* is a later epic which gives a very different picture of the reign of the Candella king, Paramardī, from that available in his own inscriptions.

of the more common form of the *vaṃśāvali* is the one from Chamba.[84]

These texts and inscriptions pertaining to past events frequently began with the origin myths of the dynasty as a preamble. Origin myths could go back to the time cycles of the Manus and relate to non-calendrical time but could also be set in the genealogical section of what I have called generational time. This serves to legitimize the founders of a dynasty by linking them with the heroes of Purāṇic ancestry. Some, however, may not resort to Purāṇic anc stry, although it tends to be brought in indirectly. By way of contrast, the narrative, as it continues in such texts, relates the succession of later rulers. This is set in a matrix of generations and of dynastic lists, emphasizes the unique event, and goes beyond the Purāṇic view of the past in, what I would like to suggest, were the major concerns perceived as important to historical change. These were primarily the recognition of the importance of acquiring caste status, the emergence of institutions linked to state formation and the establishing of new religious sects supportive of monarchy. Thus, in the Chamba *vaṃśāvali*, the origin myth merely links the earliest time with the heroes of Purāṇic ancestry. The subsequent narrative of the rulers of Chamba revolves around changes of many kinds, such as the claims to high status, the shifting of the capital to an area more conducive to revenue appropriation and administrative control, the making of grants, the introduction of Vaiṣṇavism, and so on. The chronology is what we would recognize as historical. Categories of time demarcate the earlier story from the later narrative. Such 'devices of temporal distancing' also provide indications of how the past was perceived.[85]

[84] J. Ph. Vogel, *Antiquities of Chamba State*, Calcutta 1911, 82 ff.
[85] Fabian, 31.

# VIII

## Eschatology

New chronological forms did not result in a new eschatology at the beginning and end of creation. For this, the cyclic theory continued to be the basis of cosmological time and for the larger time bracket the conditions of the Kaliyuga were referred to.[86] Elements of the eschatology of linear time do occur even within the broadly cyclic, but there is, for example, no single deity controlling time as in the Semitic religions. Time itself is sometimes projected as a deity. Time was a creator begetting heaven and earth, and that which was and that which shall be.[87] Time could be the ultimate cause.[88] The past, present and future are woven across space like warp and woof.[89] Time was imperishable and was said to encompass creation but since it was a deity it could also bring about destruction.[90] An even more evocative image describes time as *asya lokayantrasya sūtradhāraḥ*, literally, the string-holder/stage manager of this mechanism which is the universe, or that which regulates the universe.[91] However some elements of the eschatology seemed to have encouraged deviations. Among these may be noticed the variations in the structure of the cycle itself, as also the innovative idea of the coming of a saviour-figure who could intervene to change conditions and who assists in taking the cycle towards the next golden

[86] An interesting adaptation of this eschatology comes from Bali. A Balinese Hindu, Anandakusuma, asserted that the Kṛta age had recommenced in 1898. Among his reasons for saying so was that the progress of science culminating in the moon landing marked the kind of conditions which would initiate the Kṛta age. F.L. Bakker, *The Struggle of the Hindu Balinese Intellectuals*, Amsterdam 1993, 91.

[87] *Atharvaveda*, 19. 53, 1–12; 54, 1–5.

[88] *Śvetāśvatara Upaniṣad*, 1. 2. *Maitrī Upaniṣad*, 6. 15.

[89] *Bṛhadāraṇyaka Upaniṣad*, 3. 8. 3–4.

[90] *Bhagavad-gītā*, 11. 32.

[91] Bhartṛhari in *Vākyapadīya*, 3, 9, 3–5, quoted in W. Halbfass, *On Being and What There Is*, New York 1992, 205.

age. The coming of such a figure, it would seem, may not have been unrelated to the linear perceptions of time.

In Jaina cosmology, time is represented by a wheel with twelve spokes. The six ascending spokes (*utsarpiṇī*) span a period of virtue and harmony, though gradually changing, and the descending six (*avasarpiṇī*) refer to a period of increasing deterioration.[92] The two together constitute one rotation which is the equivalent of one *kalpa*. At the dawn of the Kṛta age, utopian conditions prevail. Humans are luminous and beautiful and are born as couples, giving birth to a fresh couple just before dying. The *kalpavṛkṣas* as wish-fulfilling trees satisfy all wants. There are no social distinctions, no persons in authority, no sickness or poverty. At this time Bhāratavarṣa was called *bhogabhūmi*, an epithet which changed to *karmabhūmi*, when the decline implicit in time set in.[93]

In the Buddhist concept of the wheel of time, the four ages change but without an evident break. The golden age returns and is the commencement of another cycle. A series of such cycles would seem to take the shape of a spiral and if the spiral is stretched, it approximates a more linear form. Within the larger cyclic cosmology, generational time is invoked by listing the succession of the elders of the monasteries, often co-related with segments of dynastic history. This had a bearing on succession to high office, but was also important to property rights when the monasteries became landlords. Theravāda Buddhism, as it evolved in Sri Lanka, viewed the mission of the Buddha as a unique event. Northern Buddhism had a variant on this perception in its emphasis on the saviour figure.

The saviour-figure was that of the Buddha to come, the Buddha Maitreya or 'the friendly one'. As the last Buddha, his eventual coming is referred to in the early Buddhist texts,

[92] S. Stevenson, *The Heart of Jainism*, New Delhi 1970 (rep.), 272.

[93] *Paumacariyam*, 3. 37ff: 102. 126–132. K.R. Chandra, *A Critical Study of Paumcacariyam*, Vaisali 1970, 318 ff.

but somewhat in passing.[94] Gradually the legend grew and it was said that when people became wicked and were given to violence, the Buddhist *dharma* on the decline, would be revived by Maitreya. Given the anarchy which followed this decline, people took to the forests and hid in the hills. The forest again becomes the retreat from the evils of life in the towns and villages. Ultimately, with the coming of the Buddha Maitreya, people would return and live once more in accordance with the *dharma*.[95] The past is pushed back by recalling the many Buddhas before Gautama and their long spans of time. Thus Dīpankara lived for 84,000 myriad lakhs of years a hundred thousand unaccountable *kalpas* ago. This is a timeless time and we have seen how time is negated in the spatial descriptions of the *kalpa*. The idea is firmed up by the mid-first millennium AD possibly because of the declining patronage to Buddhism among competing religions in some areas. The anticipation of a Buddha to come would shore up support for Buddhism. The Buddha Maitreya is associated with the upward movement of the wheel of time in the direction of the eventual return of the golden age. It is in effect a millennarian movement. So it is not surprising that the figures linked to the coming of the Buddha Maitreya were five hundred, one thousand or fifteen hundred years, from that of the Buddha. That Mahāyāna Buddhism in northern India was also in dialogue with Zoroastrianism, Christianity and Manichaeism could point to some rub off of millennarian ideas from these onto Buddhism. Visions of heaven and hell also became prominent in Mahāyāna Buddhist writing. Descriptions of one celestial paradise depict it as prosperous and fertile, inhabited by gods and men, and filled with fragrant flowers, singing birds and gem-trees bearing the seven gems, with lotuses which were a *yojana* in size and emitting rays, from each of which a Buddha emanated, and

[94] *Dīgha Nikāya*, 3. 75 ff.
[95] J. Legge, *The Travels of Fa-hien*, Oxford 1886, 110.

there were also vast rivers of fragrant waters — a scene of almost psychedelic glory.[96]

Millennarian and messianic ideas have more evident forms where the eschatology is linear, but they do not necessarily have to be rooted in prophetic-type religions, for the coming of the saviour can also be related to cyclic time concepts. A parallel to the Buddha Maitreya, though perhaps of a more messianic kind, was the tenth *avatāra* of Viṣṇu — Kalkin. In the *Viṣṇu Purāṇa,* the Kali age is associated with a reduction in the prevalence of *dharma,* a reversal of social norms and the exploitation by avaricious rulers of the people through taxes and other burdens. People will therefore flee to the mountains and live the life of food-gatherers. Forest dwellers had earlier, in the same chapter, been dismissed as being beyond the boundaries of caste society. However, in this case, those who had been members of a better society were reduced to a primitive existence. It is curious that this retreat of the population into subsistance seems to be the contrastive pre-condition to the return of the golden age, in both Buddhist and Brahmanical visions of the future.

The *Viṣṇu Purāṇa* states that the coming of Kalkin will occur towards the end of the Kaliyuga and will usher in the new cycle beginning with the age of virtue. He will destroy the *mlecchas,* the low-caste rulers and the heretics, and re-establish the authority of the *brāhmaṇas.*[97] He will of course be a *brāhmaṇa* himself ! The Kaliyuga is recognized as being different from other ages and requiring the constant intercession of Viṣṇu in various *avatāras.* The compassionate tone of the Buddha Maitreya story contrasts sharply with the strident voice predicting the coming of Kalkin. Perhaps the difference lay in the restoration of the Buddhist *dharma* being the primary purpose of the coming of Maitreya, whereas Kalkin's concern was also to restore power and wealth to the upper castes.

[96] *Sukhāvatīvyuha,* 15 ff. For a discussion of the rationale of the particular seven gems, see Xinru Liu, *Ancient India and Ancient China,* Delhi 1988, 53ff.

[97] *Viṣṇu Purāṇa* 4. 24. 98ff.

In all these eschatologies, the golden age is at the beginning of the cycle and in some it returns when the cycle is completed and the next one begins. Descriptions of these utopias do not suggest the need for effort and labour. Thus in a Buddhist text, it is said of the Uttara-Kurus that they claimed no possessions either of wealth or of women, nor did they need to cultivate the land, for ripened grain was always naturally available.[98] Elsewhere the earth itself was said to be edible, or there were wish-fulfilling trees which provided all needs. But when the decline set in and utopian conditions diminished, the requirement for labour arose. This is associated with conflict between people over the division of society into families and access to food and fields. There is a relationship between time and the necessity to labour.[99]

A story is related in Buddhist texts about the election of the Mahāsammata — the great elected one, who became necessary in a period of decline when men and women fought over the instituting of families, over food and over the ownership of fields. The situation of constant conflict was resolved by electing a protector, and contracting rights and obligations.[100] In the Brahmanical view of the earliest age, there was neither a king nor punishment, but gradually human passions destroyed its perfection.[101] The office of the *rājā* had to be created to control the deterioration of social conditions. Here the recognition of decline does not call for the people electing a ruler but the gods appointing one and there is a contractual agreement between the appointee and the people. Utopian times are characterized by an absence of labour. The necessity to labour comes in periods of decline. Yet this is not

[98] *Dīgha Nikāya*, 3. 199, 7.

[99] E.P. Thompson, looking at the question of time and labour in a very different context, makes the point that the change brought by industrialization and capitalism introduced a new time discipline in England which moved away from traditional time. 'Time, Work, Discipline and Industrial Capitalism', *Past and Present*, 1967, 38, 56–97.

[100] *Dīgha Nikāya*, 3. 85 ff.

[101] *Mahābhārata*, Śāntiparvan, 59. 13ff.

an absolute criteria for labour, especially where labour is also linked to moral values. Those who constructed these utopias were either *brāhmaṇas* or Buddhist and Jaina monks, none of whom were labouring men. In theory the Buddhist *bhikkhu* did labour but it was of a different kind since it centred on the concerns of the renouncer and renunciation ideally abandoned or reduced to a minimum both time and labour. But then, the elimination of the need to labour is characteristic of many utopias, including the Judaeo-Christian.

Judaeo-Christian eschatology propounded the initial paradise of the garden of Eden and the trajectory of time terminated with the paradise in heaven, at least for those fortunate enough to have a judgement in their favour. This was a rejection of the earlier cyclic theory of the ancient Greeks. Medieval Christian theology was averse to cyclical theories. Only the Greek concept of eternity with its endless duration of seamless time, enters Christian eschatology.[102] Yet curiously, in the modern transposing of linear time as an essential component of historical consciousness, the cyclic cosmology of the Greeks was segregated from their historical writing. In this case, cyclic time was not seen as negating history. Thus, a refusal of history through recourse to cyclic time was identified more frequently with colonial cultures.

This might explain the reluctance and even the dismissal of attempts to enquire into how these concepts of time were constructed, after the failure of the initial attempts to comprehend them. H.H. Wilson, among the more respected Indologists of the nineteenth century, commenting on the description of time in the *Viṣṇu Purāṇa*, makes a telling statement. 'It does not seem necessary to refer the invention (of time) to any astronomical computations or to any attempt to represent actual chronology.'[103]

Had the initial enquiry been pursued, the links between astronomical computations and the grand design of cyclic

[102] R. Sorabji, *Time, Creation and the Continuum*, London 1983, 98ff; 182ff.
[103] *Viṣṇu Purāṇa*, trans. H.H. Wilson, 22, n.4.

time as well as the more mundane time reckonings of historical chronology would have become more visible. The shading away of myth from history was also sometimes articulated in categories of time. The simultaneous use of different categories of time is symbolic of registering historical change and priorities in historical functioning. These differentiations, it seems to me, are significant, not merely because we in the twentieth century are analysing past concepts of time, but because there was a reason in the past for making these differentiations.

The characterizing of societies as using either cyclic or linear time is an inadequate explanation for the centrality or otherwise of history. Research, even into European history, has endorsed various categories of historical time and to that extent has distanced itself from the earlier single category. Time, as conceived in cosmology or eschatology, does not exclude the use of other categories of time and these can be simultaneous in the same society. It seems more appropriate to enquire into how a society uses a particular category and what is being intended by that use. Thus the statements which each form of time reckoning are making are not identical. The inclusion of cyclic time is not a characteristic of cultures which are historically stunted but an indication of historical complexity. This complexity is reflected in the perceptions of the past in pre-modern times, the premises of which were different from the writing of history today.

This attempt at an exploration of time and history is not just an exercise in intellectual curiosity. In questioning the presuppositions about societies and cultures as they have been conceptualized in the historiography of recent times, it becomes necessary to enquire into many facets of the past. I have tried to argue that even concepts of time in early India, as read by earlier scholars, need to be interpreted afresh. Our readings both of time and of history have undergone mutations. But the metaphor remains.

# Bibliography

## PRIMARY SOURCES


Alberuni. Sachau, E.C. (trans.), *Alberuni's India*, Delhi 1964 (reprint).

*Alhā-Khaṇḍa*, Waterfield, W., *The Lay of Alha*, Gurgaon 1990 (reprint).

*Aṅguttara-nikāya*, Morris, R. and Hardy, E. (eds.), P.T.S., London 1976 (reprint).

Arrian, *Indika*, McCrindle, J.W. (trans.), *Ancient India as Described by Megasthenes and Arrian*, London 1877.

*Atharva Veda Saṁhitā*, Vishvabandhu (ed.), Hoshiarpur 1960–2.

*Baudhāyana Dharma-sūtra*, Hultzsch, E. (ed.), Leipzig 1884.

*Bhagavad-gītā*, Zaehner, R.C. (ed.), *The Bhagavad-gītā*, Oxford 1975 (reprint).

Bloch, J., *Les Inscriptions d'Asoka*, Paris 1950.

Chandbardai, *Pṛthvirājarāso*, Mohan Singh (ed.), Udaipur 1965.

*Dīgha-nikāya*, Rhys Davids, T.W. *et al.* (eds.), P.T.S., London 1975 (reprint).

*Epigraphia Indica.*

Fa-Hien. Legge J., *The Travels of Fâ-hien*, Oxford 1886.

Kalhaṇa, *Rājataraṅginī*, Stein, M.A. (ed.), London 1892; (trans.) London 1900.

*Kauṭilīya, Arthaśāstra*, Kangle, R.P. (ed. and trans.), University of Bombay, 1965.

*Mahābhārata*, Sukthankar, V.S. *et al.* (eds.), B.O.R.I., Poona 1933.

*Manu Dharma Śāstra*, Motwani, K. (ed.), Madras 1959 (trans.) Bühler, G., *The Laws of Manu*, Varanasi 1967 (reprint).

*Matsya Purāṇa*, Poona, Anandasram Sanskrit Series, 1907.

*Paumacariyam*, Jacobi, H., (ed.) Varanasi 1962.

Pliny, *Natural History*, London 1938.

*Ṛg Veda Saṃhitā*, Max Müller F. (ed.), Varanasi 1966 (reprint).

*Saṃyutta-nikāya*, Rhys Davids, C. and Woodward, F.L. (trans.), P.T.S., London 1918–30.

*Śatapatha Brāhmaṇa*, 5 vols., L.V.S. Press, Bombay 1940.

*Upaniṣads*. Radhakrishnan, S., (ed.) *The Principal Upaniṣads*, London 1953.

Varāhamihira, *Bṛhatsaṁhitā*, M. Ramakrishna Bhat (ed.), Varanasi 1981.

*Viṣṇu Purāṇa*, Gita Press, Gorakhpur, V.S. 1990.

Wilson, H.H. (trans.), *Vishnu Purana*, Calcutta 1961.

## SECONDARY SOURCES

### *Articles*

Bentley, J., 'Remarks on the Principal Eras and Dates of the Ancient Hindus', *Asiatic Researches*, 1808, vol. 8, 315ff.

———, 'On the Hindu System of Astronomy', *Asiatic Researches*, London 1809, vol. 8., 195ff.

Bivar, A. D. H., 'The Azes Era and the Indravarma Casket', *South Asian Archaeology, 1979*, Berlin 1981, pp. 369–76.

Cardona, G., 'A Path Still Taken: Some Early Indian Arguments', *Journal of the American Oriental Society*, New York, 1991, 3, 3, pp. 445–64.

Colebrooke, H., 'Hindu Astronomy', *Asiatic Journal*, 1826, 21, 360ff.

Davies, S., 'On the Indian Cycle of Sixty Years', *Asiatic Researches*, 1794, vol. 3, 289ff.

Eliade, M., 'Time and Eternity in Indian Thought', *Man in Time*, Princeton University, New Jersery, Bollinger series xxx, p. 3.

Fleet, J. F., 'The Kaliyuga of 3102 BC', *Journal of the Royal Asiatic Society of Great Britain and Ireland*, 1911, pp. 479–96, and 675–98.

Fussman, G., 'Nouvelles inscriptions Śaka: ère d'Eucratide, ère d'Azes, ère Vikrama, ère de Kaniṣka', *BEFEO*, 1980, 67, pp. 1–43.

Inden, R., 'Orientalist Construction of India', *Modern Asian Studies,* 1986, 20, 3, pp. 401–46.

Jones, William, 'The Third Discourse', *Asiatic Researches,* vol. 1, 1789, p. 354.

Kielhorn, F., 'Examination of Questions Connected with the Vikram Era', *The Indian Antiquary,* 1891, 20, pp. 397–414.

Krishan, Y., 'The Astronomical Revolution in India about AD 400 and its Implications', *Vishveshvaranand Indological Journal,* Hoshiarpur, 1977, 15, 2, pp. 265–84.

Nakamura, H., 'Time in Indian and Japanese Thought', in Fraser, J.T. (ed.), *The Voices of Time,* London, 1986.

Perera, L.H., 'The Pali Chronicles of Ceylon', in Philips, C.H., (ed.) *Historians of India, Pakistan and Ceylon,* London 1961.

Pingree, D., 'Astronomy and Astrology in India and Iran', *ISIS,* 1963, 54, 2, pp. 176, 229–46.

———, 'The Purāṇas and Jyotiḥśāstra: Astronomy', *Journal of the American Oriental Society,* 1990, 110, 2, p. 275.

Sen, S.N., 'Astronomy', in Bose, D.M. *et al.* (eds.), *A Concise History of Science in India,* New Delhi, 1971. p, 81.

Sukhthankar, V.S., 'The Bhṛgus and the Bhārata, a Text Historical Study', *Annals of the Bhandarkar Oriental Research Institute,* 18, pp. 1–76.

Thapar, Romila, 'Genealogical Patterns as Perceptions of the Past', *Studies in History,* 1971, N.S. 7,1, pp.1–36.

———, 'Society and Historical Consciousness: the Itihāsa-Purāṇa Tradition', in Bhattacharya, S. and Thapar, Romila (eds.), *Situating Indian History,* Delhi 1986, pp. 353–83.

Thompson, E.P., 'Time, Work, Discipline and Industrial Capitalism', *Past and Present,* 1967, 38, pp. 56–97.

Wilford, F., 'On the Chronology of the Hindus', *Asiatic Researches,* vol. 5, 1808, 241 ff.

Woodburn, J., 'Egalitarian Societies', *Man,* N.S. 1982, 17, pp. 431–51.

## MONOGRAPHS

Bakker, F. L., *The struggles of the Hindu Balinese Intellectuals,* Amsterdam, 1993.

Balslev, A. N., *A Study of Time in Indian Philosophy*, Wiesbaden, 1983.
Basham, A. L., *The Wonder that Was India*, London 1954.
———, *History and Doctrine of the Ājīvikas*, London 1951.
Bechert, H. (ed.), *The Dating of the Historical Buddha*, 2 vols., Göttingen 1991.
Bhattacharya, S. and Thapar, Romila (eds.), *Situating Indian History*, Delhi 1986.
Bose, D. M. *et al.* (eds.), *A Concise History of Science in India*, New Delhi 1971.
Chandra, K.R., *A Critical Study of Paumacariyam*, Vaisali 1970.
Coomaraswamy, A.K., *Time and Eternity*, Ascona 1947.
Cumont, F., *Astrology and Religion among Greeks and Romans*, New York, 1960 (reprint).
Eliade, M., *Cosmos and History: the Myth of the Eternal Return*, New York 1959.
Fabian, J., *Time and the Other*, New York 1983.
Fraser, J.T., *The Voices of Time*, London 1986.
Ghosh, A. (ed.), *Jaina Art and Architecture*, 3 vols., New Delhi 1974–5.
Goldman, R.P., *Gods, Priests and Warriors*, New York 1977.
Halbfass, W., *On Being and What There Is*, New York 1977.
Kane, P.V., *History of Dharmaśāstra*, vols. 1--5, Poona 1958.
Lambert, W.G. and Millard, A.R., *Atrahasis*, Oxford 1969.
Liu Xinru, *Ancient India and Ancient China*, Delhi 1988.
Mandal, K. K., *A Comparative Study of the Concepts of Space and Time in Indian Thought*, Varanasi 1968.
Mill, James, *The History of British India*, vol. 1, London 1958, 5th ed.
Mitchiner, J.E., *The Yuga Purāṇa*, Delhi 1986.
Norman Brown, W., *Man in the Universe*, Berkeley 1966.
Pargiter, F.E., *The Purāna Texts of the Dynasties of the Kali Age*, Delhi 1975 (reprint).
———, *Ancient Indian Historical Tradition*, London 1922.
Pathak, V.S., *Ancient Historians of India*, Bombay 1966.
Philips, C.H., (ed.) *Historians of India, Pakistan and Ceylon*, London 1961.

Pingree, D., *Yavanajātaka of Sphujidhvaja*, Cambridge Mass., 1978.

———, *Jyotiḥśāstra*, Wiesbaden 1981.

Schnabel, P., *Berossos und die Babylonisch-Hellenistische Literatur*, Leipzig 1923.

Schwab, R., *La Renaissance Orientale*, Paris 1950.

Sircar, D.C., *Studies in the Yuga Purāṇa and Other Texts*, Delhi 1964.

———, *Indian Epigraphy*, Delhi 1965.

Sorabji, R., *Time, Creation and the Continuum*, London 1983.

Stevenson, S., *The Heart of Jainism*, Delhi 1970 (reprint).

Thapar, Romila, *Clans, Caste and Origin Myths in Early India*, Simla 1992.

———, *From Lineage to State*, Delhi 1984.

Toulmin, S. and Goodfield, J., *The Discovery of Time*, Harmondsworth 1967.

Vogel, J. Ph., *Antiquities of Chamba State*, Calcutta 1911.

Warder, A.K., *An Introduction to Indian Historiography*, Bombay 1972.

# Index